Eliane Fernandes Pietrovski
Elton Ivan Schneider
Dalcio R. dos Reis

Strategy and Innovation

Eliane Fernandes Pietrovski
Elton Ivan Schneider
Dalcio R. dos Reis

Strategy and Innovation

Teaching case in Brazilian small business

ScienciaScripts

Imprint

Any brand names and product names mentioned in this book are subject to trademark, brand or patent protection and are trademarks or registered trademarks of their respective holders. The use of brand names, product names, common names, trade names, product descriptions etc. even without a particular marking in this work is in no way to be construed to mean that such names may be regarded as unrestricted in respect of trademark and brand protection legislation and could thus be used by anyone.

Cover image: www.ingimage.com

This book is a translation from the original published under ISBN 978-613-9-63426-2.

Publisher:
Sciencia Scripts
is a trademark of
Dodo Books Indian Ocean Ltd. and OmniScriptum S.R.L publishing group

120 High Road, East Finchley, London, N2 9ED, United Kingdom
Str. Armeneasca 28/1, office 1, Chisinau MD-2012, Republic of Moldova, Europe
Printed at: see last page
ISBN: 978-620-7-66629-4

SUMMARY

PRESENTATION

Entrepreneurship and staying competitive is a challenge to be faced, especially for Brazil's micro and small technology-based companies.

It is necessary to adopt strategies for national and international markets, with the help of new product technologies and management processes.

The case to be studied seeks to analyse the development of the strategic management and innovation process in a small technology-based company in Brazil, through the application of discussions on the schools of strategic planning and from the perspective of theory, which discuss the relationships in which organisations adapt their strategy and organisational structure to the environmental context in which they are inserted.

This is a case study whose factors of analysis allow us to identify the innovative performance of a small company that originated from technology-based entrepreneurship, which went through the stages of business development, pre-incubation, incubation and acceleration, all of which were linked to a Technological Innovation Incubator at a university in Brazil.

The analysis will allow us to identify the entrepreneur's management traits when faced with business opportunities, as well as the paths that led him to adopt innovative strategies when faced with a challenge between entrepreneurship and competitiveness.

This case highlights the inferences of a business idea, from its conception to its realisation, as well as its expectations and future challenges, in the search for strategies that will perpetuate the company's competitive edge.

The main results of the analysis of the selected company identify the entrepreneur's management traits in the face of business opportunities.

The manager has the capacity for effective organisational adaptation, not only to foresee and implement new forms of management processes, but also to manage people and the company's internal controls.

The adaptive model studied offers a theory that allowed the company to be understood and analysed. It can be concluded that the management style of small businesses is more flexible, adapting to the characteristics and reality of the market encountered, and the whole must be analysed to identify the most striking characteristics.

This teaching case can be applied in undergraduate and postgraduate Lato Senso courses to develop students' ability to analyse problem situations and synthesise them in the light of the theories proposed, in the discussion of business opportunities for new entrepreneurs, in the identification of characteristics that refute or confirm the theory under discussion; in the ability to make relationships between the theories analysed, indicating points of commonality and points of divergence.

CHAPTER 1

INTRODUCTION

Entrepreneurship studies follow two main streams of research. One focuses on the economy and the innovative impact of entrepreneurs on economic development. Schumpeter (1961) was the forerunner in the approach to the role of the entrepreneur as an agent of **"creative destruction", of the** economy in static equilibrium, eliminating obsolete products and processes through the innovative process which leads to economic and social development. The other stream of researchers involves studies of entrepreneurial behaviour, seeking to identify certain psychological traits, verify the social environments in which they operate and other particular factors or characteristics that determine a pattern for analysis.

These studies include McClelland's (1965) theory of motivations, among others, which identified factors related to the need for personal fulfilment and the motivation to carry out an entrepreneurial activity as fundamental to the process. In order to carry out entrepreneurial activities as well as systematic innovation, Drucker (2014) states that it is necessary to have discipline in the search for opportunities for change, as innovation needs to be seen as planned, organised, **systematic and rational** work, **"what the** innovator sees and learns needs to be subjected to **rigorous logical analysis" (DRUCKER, 2014, p.67).**

For this study, the discussions on the schools of strategic planning proposed by Mintzberg et al (2009) are applied, especially the school of organisational configuration and the adaptive model of Miles and Snow (1978), according to which organisations adapt their strategy and organisational structure to the environmental context in which they are inserted. The case to be studied, in the light of Miles and Snow's (1978) theory, is EXA Automação Industrial, a small technology-based company, which came out of the pre-incubation, incubation and acceleration processes, linked to the Entrepreneurship and Innovation Programme (PROEM) of the Technological Innovation Incubator (IUT-PG) at the Ponta Grossa Campus of the Federal Technological University of Paraná.

This study sought to analyse the development of the strategic management and innovation process at EXA. In order to identify how the strategic decisions of a small technology-based company can be explained in the light of Miles and Snow's adaptive cycle theory, the following questions were raised:

    a) The characteristic of the entrepreneur in the search for the technical and economic viability of the company indicates which management style? Reactive, Defender, Analytical or Prospector?

    b) Can the company's strategic decisions be explained in the light of Miles and Snow's adaptive cycle theory?

c) When analysing the decisions from the point of view of the adaptive cycle (Entrepreneur, Engineering and Structure) in comparison with the management style (Reactive, Defender, Analytical, Prospector) can it be said that a single style was adopted? Has the management style changed in the different stages of the cycle?

d) Is there alignment between the chosen strategy and the organisational processes and structures?

Miles and Snow's (1978) model presents a typology to be adopted by small and medium-sized companies, as a counterpoint to Michael Porter's strategies (Cost Strategy, Differentiation Strategy and Focus Strategy) traditionally applied to large organisations.

CHAPTER 2

THE EXA CASE

A young student called Theodoro, from the Industrial Automation Technology course, when introduced to Entrepreneurship, one of the subjects on the course and with the encouragement of some teachers, had a dream of setting up his own business:

> How can I differentiate myself in the labour market, or better still, how can I be the owner of my own business, working in the field of industrial automation? How can I make the most of all these years of study, given that I identify with the area I chose to study?
>
> Theodoro Bahniuk Neto

The name Theodoro comes from the Greek and means given by God. Perhaps that's where our protagonist's ability to always help his neighbour comes from, solving problems and finding solutions based on the skills he developed in his technical course.

Theodoro's entrepreneurial career (FIGURE 1) begins with his admission to university (2004), the approval of his project at the Technology Incubator (2006/2007), the creation of the company EXA (2009), the development of the first wafer-making machine (2010), the approval of his project at the Ecotechnology Park (2011), the development of a fully automated wafer-making machine (2013), the construction of his company headquarters (2015) and the acquisition of more companies: Atto (2016) and B2 and Dunamys (2017) and most recently the acquisition of the company Zetta (2018).

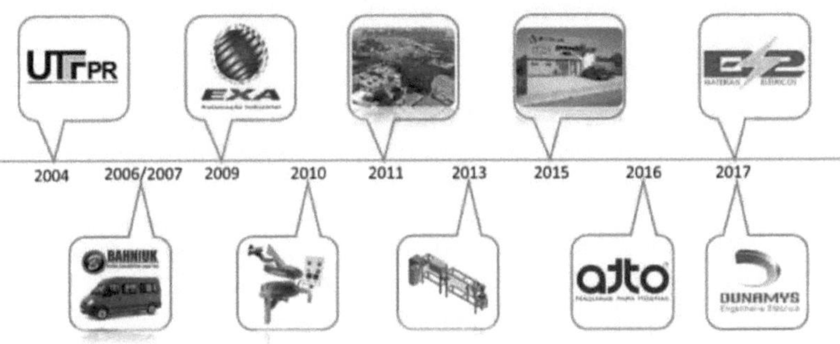

Figura 1 - Timeline: from project to realisation
Source: Images provided by the entrepreneur.

From the dream of a young man, a Technologist in Industrial Automation (2007), a Specialist in Industrial Mechatronics (2009) and an Electrical Engineer (2014), EXA was born, a company in the field of electronic automation in the city of Ponta Grossa, Paraná - Brazil. The name EXA was chosen because it represents a prefix from the International System of Units that denotes a factor of 10^{18} , thus characterising the growth of the idea of a project from academia to the market, as highlighted by the press (FIGURE 2).

Figura 2 - Articles published by newspapers and television networks

Even in the name EXA, you can see a desire for great achievements. Theodoro endeavours to seize life's opportunities without losing his sense of reality, and while he knows how to aim for the infinite, he always seeks originality, creativity and innovation in any task.

CHAPTER 3

ORIGIN

EXA was the result of the Course Conclusion Work (TCC) in Industrial Automation Technology at the Federal Technological University of Paraná, Ponta Grossa Campus (UTFPR-PG), in 2007.

The entrepreneur is Theodoro Bahniuk Neto and his final assignment was to develop an automatic door system for student and staff transport vans (FIGURE 3 and FIGURE 4).

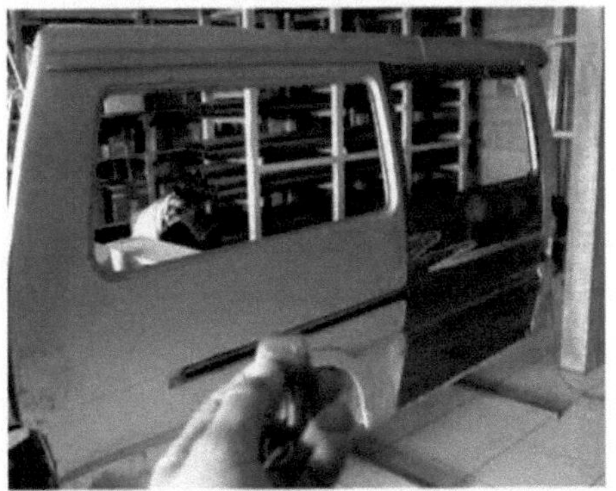

Figura 3   **- Prototype of the Automatic Door Project for Vans**

Source: Image provided by the entrepreneur.

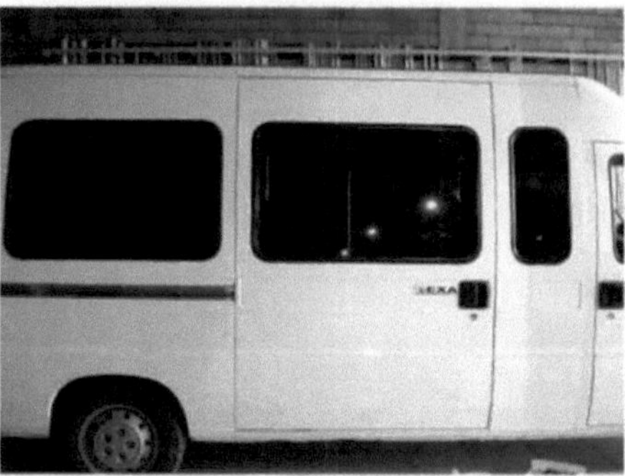

Figura 4 - Automatic door for vans
Source: Images provided by the entrepreneur.

Like any young entrepreneur, Theodoro encountered several obstacles in getting his idea off the ground, such as inexperience in business management, a lack of capital to start a business, a lot of desire and still little rationality in what he wanted to do, as he didn't know how to run a business or even what effective paths he should take. In this sense, when he learned about the support work of UTFPR-PG's Entrepreneurship and Innovation Programme (PROEM), especially in the area of management, Theodoro saw the programme as an opportunity to develop his entrepreneurial side; after all, at PROEM he would have the support of professors in the area of management and engineering to help him improve his business idea. As a result, he submitted his business pre-project to the project evaluation board, which was favourably received.

pre-incubation period at the UTFPR Technology Hotel (HT-PG). The first step towards transforming their business idea, the result of their final year thesis, into reality was therefore taken.

From the dream world to the real world

Like most entrepreneurs, when Theodoro presented his project to PROEM, he faithfully believed that his business idea was viable and that it was an opportunity that only he had visualised. After a year of studying aspects such as technical feasibility, economic viability and drawing up a business plan for the van door system, Theodoro realised that there was already a product similar to his on the domestic market, and worst of all, at a low price and cost. The initial dream of EXA van door systems was over, but not the dream of his own business.

What's next? The dream of owning your own business seemed so far from reality...

But the young man, a follower of Christian principles, was predestined to follow the path of faith. Very religious, Theodoro found an opportunity in the church he attended that he hadn't seen

10

before: the refurbishment of host-making machines. Because the machines are imported and have no technical assistance in Brazil, when they have problems, they sit idle and cannot be used. At the request of the church's parish priest, Theodoro maintains the machines, changes parts and improves them, and soon realises that there are other churches with the same problem. A new light is switched on at the end of the tunnel, but this time will it be a divine light?

The fresh start

Leaving his first project behind, Theodoro moved on to new ideas and solutions in the field of industrial automation. After providing automation services to convents and seminaries in the city and region, the entrepreneur realised that this activity could also be offered to other companies in the region.

From the friendship that arose with the Catholic sisters responsible for making communion wafers, who always sought him out and admired him for his willingness to serve, carrying out not only repairs to the machines used to make communion wafers (FIGURE 5) but also collaborating on other tasks in the convents, such as small repairs to electrical and electronic equipment in general.

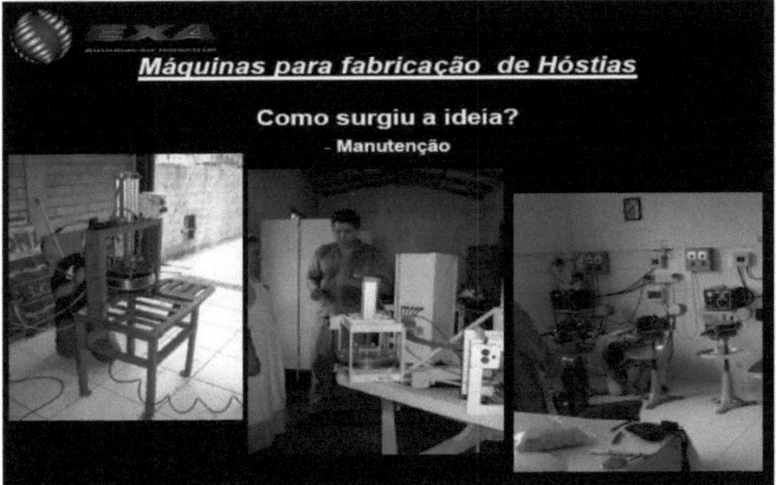

Figura 5   - Maintenance on wafer-making machines
Source: Images provided by the entrepreneur.

According to Theodoro Bahniuk Neto:

In 2006, during an internship at a local company, working in the technical area, I started servicing wafer-making machines in monasteries and convents and as I had learnt how to make a good business plan, I decided to develop one specifically for wafer machines. This product worked so well that today we have sold our machines to several states in Brazil, from Amazonas to Rio Grande do Sul.

Two companies currently manufacture these types of machines in Brazil, one in São Paulo and the other our company.

According to an article published on the website www.terra.com on 13/03/2013, the Catholic Church has 1.285 billion faithful worldwide, of which 40% are in Latin America, and in Brazil there are more than 172 million faithful (Chart 1).

As well as bringing together a large number of faithful, the Catholic Church also presents itself as a congregation with a wide range of activities, involving schools, universities, hospitals and nursing homes, which, due to its worldwide operations, can be considered a large multinational corporation.

As a result, Theodoro realised that this was a little-explored niche and turned his attention to designing a machine to make communion wafers from domestic parts, at a low cost and with production on a large scale, with the potential market being the more than 10,800 parishes in Brazil, whose profit margins on the sale of communion wafers can reach 300%, see Table 01. Based on these findings, technical and economic feasibility studies were resumed and a business plan was drawn up during the pre-incubation period, which lasted until 2009.

Table 1 - The numbers of the Catholic Church

Catholics	1.285.000.000
Fathers	412.236
Faithful for a priest	2.900
Bishops	5.104
Nursery schools	70,544 (6,478,627 children)
Primary schools	92,847 (31,151,170 students)
Secondary schools	43,591 (17,793,559 students)
University students	3.338.455
Hospitals	5.305
Asylums	17.223
The Catholic Church in Brazil*	
Number of faithful	172.200.000
Number of Parishes	10.802
Host consumption by parish	37,000 units/month**
Annual consumption (approx.)	5.800.000.000
Estimated Margin	300%***

Sources[*] : *Anuaruim Statisticum Ecclesiae* -Vatican (2015).

---

[1] * http://www.paulinas.org.br/radio/pt-br/?system=news&id=4591&action=read
** Data provided by Fábrica Nossa Senhora de Fátima, in a report on the UOL website, available at :http://economia.uol.com.br/noticias/redacao/2013/07/26/fabrica-faz-hostia-turning-sweet-and-treating-with-a-speech therapist.htm

The process for making communion wafers is simple (FIGURE 6) and consists of four stages: mixing flour and water, baking, moistening the disc formed by the dough and cutting it to standard size.

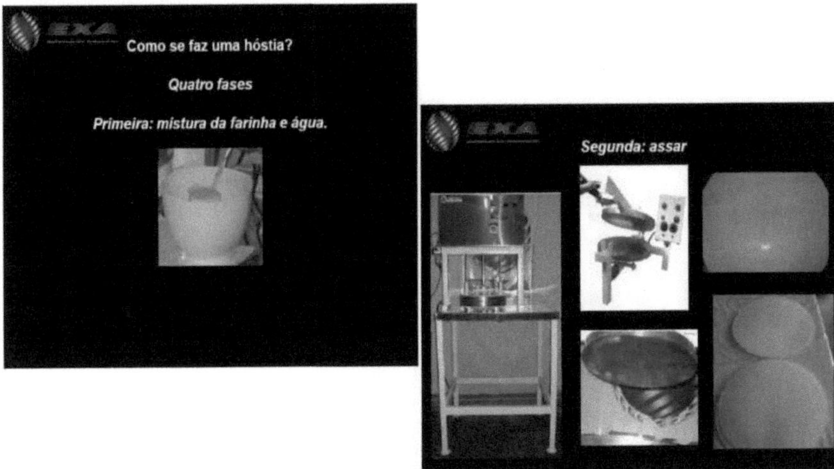

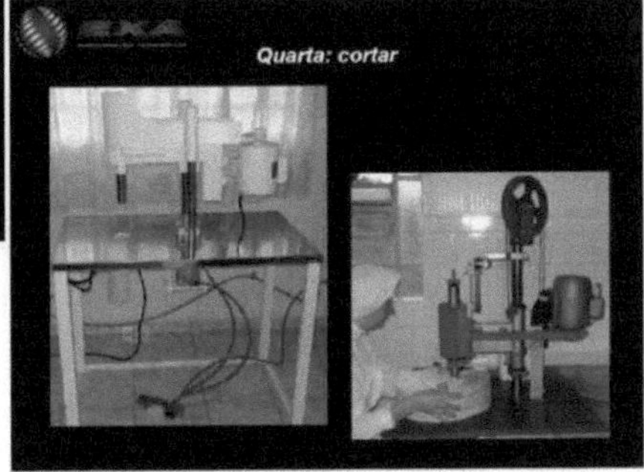

Figura 6   - Process for making communion wafers

Source: Images provided by the entrepreneur.

As the idea for the project strengthened and the work carried out at the conventions and seminars, the need arose to form a company to move on to another phase of expanding the idea, only

---

*** http://pegntv.globo.com/Pegn/0,6993,LIR332690-5027,00.html
http://noticias.terra.com.br/mundo/europa/renuncia-do-papa/igreja-catolica-em-numeros-12- billion-royals-40-in-america-latina,d8908d780eb5d310VgnVCM3000009acceb0aRCRD.html

now at the UTFPR Innovation Incubator (IUT-PG). Thus, the company EXA was founded in July 2009 and completed the acceleration phase at IUT-PG.

That's how the light came to be!

From prototype to product realisation (FIGURE 7).

Produto

Figura 7   - Host-making machine

Source: Image provided by the entrepreneur.

Theodoro began his work in a small area next to his parents' house, and with just two collaborators, he built the wafer-making machine, which was no longer just a project on paper, it was a reality, almost a divine inspiration. In 2010, the wafer-making machines followed the process shown in Figure 8.

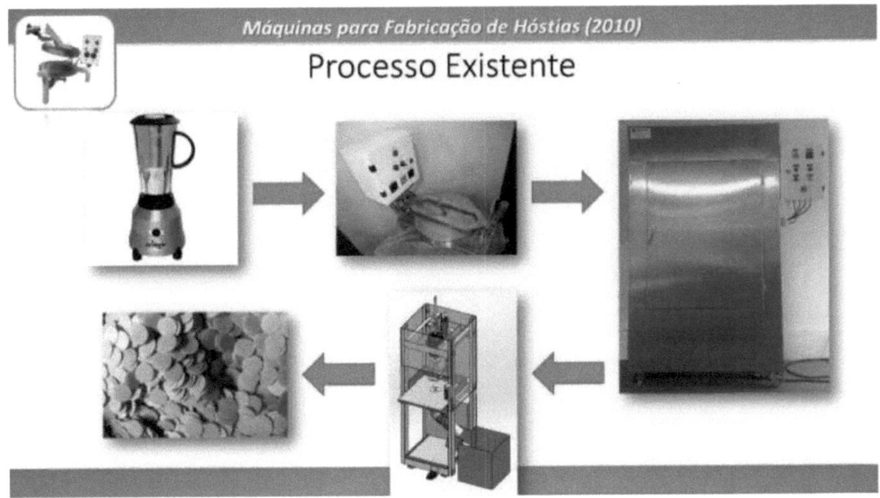

Figura 8 - Process for making communion wafers
Source: Image provided by the entrepreneur.

As a service provider, an activity that EXA continues to carry out, but now as a machine manufacturer, we are not yet talking about the **"production-line machine", but rather** EXA's first **automated wafer-cutting press** (FIGURE 9).

Figure 9 - Stamping and roller cutting
Source: Image provided by the entrepreneur.

CHAPTER 4

EXA - A GROWING MARKET

EXA, in 2010, is a concrete reality, as the first EXA wafer-making machine is already available and in operation, although it doesn't yet fulfil the initial idea of an automated production machine-line, but it does meet current market demands (FIGURE 10).

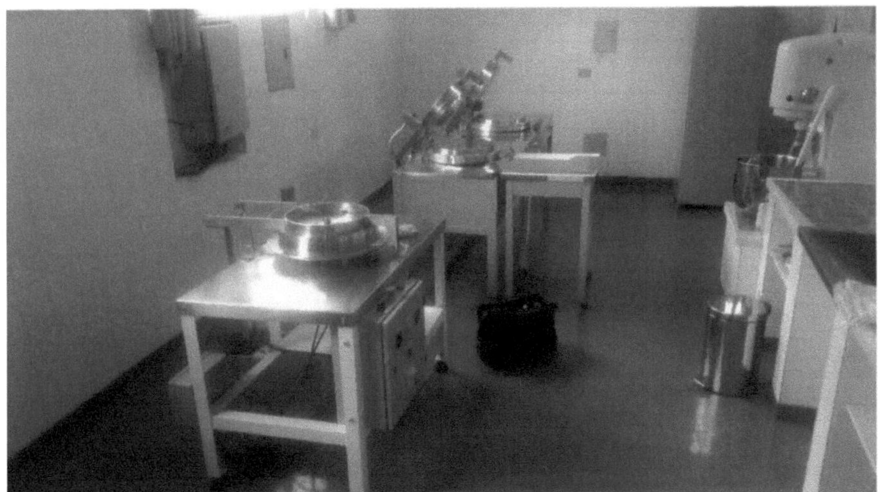

Figure 10 - Customised machine

Source: Image provided by the entrepreneur.

Due to the worldwide demand for the production of unconsecrated communion wafers and the fact that the vast majority of production is handmade, there is currently a great opportunity in the national and international market to develop an automated line to manufacture communion wafers. To this end, EXA came up with the idea of developing a machine that covers the entire process, i.e. mixing the flour and water, baking the sheets, cutting, packaging and inspecting the quality of the finished product, considerably increasing productivity, increasing the competitiveness of the supplier manufacturer for customers, and guaranteeing food safety. The stages were carried out at different times, leading to production contamination, low productivity and expensive equipment.

The dream and the technical and economic feasibility projects continue!

Theodoro intends to expand its operations physically in the future. In 2011, EXA, with the support of the IUT-PG Incubator, had a project approved for its future installation in the Ecotechnological Park in the city of Ponta Grossa - PR, Brazil (FIGURE 11).In order to make the new project viable, Theodoro and EXA have the support of the City Council, with regard to the real estate incentives of donating the physical space; the exemption from Property Tax (IPTU) for 10 (ten) years; the 50% reduction in the rate of Service Tax (ISS), as defined in the specific municipal law. This special incentive is aimed at technology-based companies and support activities, which must be approved by the Ecotechnological Park Development Council - CONDEPARQUE, and which can represent the integrated development of the municipality, due to the creation of new jobs, the use of local raw materials and market possibilities.

Figure 11 - Ecotechnological Park
Source: Images provided by the entrepreneur

The land area is 1,500m^2 , with a total area to be built of approximately 500m^2 (FIGURE 12), which is expected to generate more jobs in the city.

Figure 12 - Project for future installation in the Ecotechnological Park

Source: Image provided by the entrepreneur

Seeing a new market opportunity, Theodoro set about developing a new product idea, **a "production-line machine"** for the automated manufacture of communion wafers. Based on the data he had obtained about the market, he set out to find out who the current machine manufacturers were and where they were located. Because the existing factories in Latin America (Mexico) and Europe (Italy, Spain and Germany) were using obsolete technology, not investing in innovation, with machines that were difficult to maintain and, above all, had low productivity, as well as high transport costs to the domestic market and South America in general. Theodoro realised that the idea of equipment with national technology was promising. What's more, the development of machinery and equipment to improve the production process of small and micro industries fits in perfectly with metalworking.

In order to make the project viable, Theodoro once again faced the challenge of obtaining financial resources to make his wafer production line technically viable, even though the company was up and running. So he drew up a project (FIGURE 13) to apply for funds from funding agencies such as the Araucária Foundation, the Federation of Industries of Paraná (FIEP), the Paraná Institute of Technology (TECPAR) and the Financier of Studies and Projects (FINEP), a Brazilian public company that promotes science, technology and innovation in companies, universities, technological institutes and other public or private institutions.

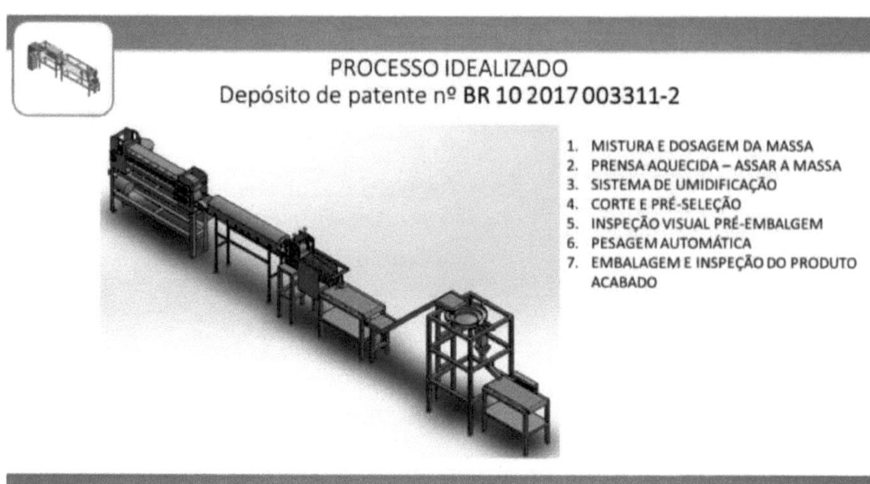

Figura 13 - Tecnova Project

Source: Image provided by the entrepreneur.

The project presented to the development agencies involved: (i) hiring a management and planning consultancy; (ii) developing the design and operating control command for the wafer machine; (iii) *networking* with suppliers and partners; (iv) adapting the physical facilities; and (v) acquiring equipment and technology, taking into account the possibilities of outsourcing services and components.

EXA had its innovation project approved in Public Call 21/2013, of the Programme to Support Innovation in Micro and Small Companies in the State of Paraná (Tecnova), for a total of R$324,637.00 (FIGURE 14).

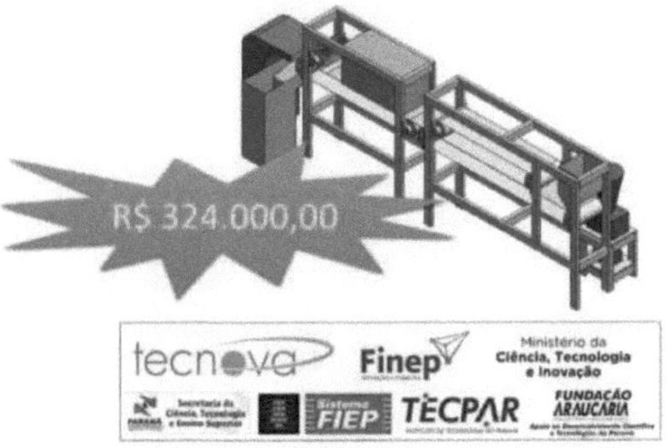

Figura 14   - Tecnova project approved

Source: Images provided by the entrepreneur.

Theodoro highlights the project:

> EXA was one of 64 companies chosen out of 220 in the state of Paraná, and the only one in the city of Ponta Grossa. Our project consisted of making a continuous line for manufacturing communion wafers and the result allowed us to file a worldwide patent.

This programme is an initiative of the Federal Government, through the Financier of Studies and Projects/Ministry of Science, Technology, Innovation and Communication (FINEP/MCTIC), which focuses on supporting technological innovation and micro and small businesses. In Paraná, the Araucária Foundation carries out the programme's actions in partnership with the Federation of Industries of Paraná (FIEP) and the Paraná Institute of Technology (TECPAR), under the coordination of the State Secretariat for Science, Technology and Higher Education (SETI).

The "machine-production line" project **for the automated manufacture of communion** wafers was realised by Theodoro (FIGURE 15). Through this project, a major improvement in the company's structure and tooling was possible, as various pieces of equipment and **software** were acquired with the help of the programme, such as: lathe, milling machine, **SolidWorks**. In addition to other items purchased with the company's own resources: **workstation** for projects, **Eplan Electric,** manual hydraulic forklift, MIG welding machine. All these resources were fundamental, not only for meeting the programme's targets, but also for the growth of the company as a whole, from training the technical team to improving manufacturing processes.

Figura 15   - Machine production line
Source: Image provided by the entrepreneur.

When it comes to intellectual protection policy, the entrepreneur emphasises the importance of registering all his companies' trademarks. Exa has filed Patent No. PI0803988-7A2 for the process of making bale separators from reforested wood. As for intellectual property rights that can be protected, it has a contract with UTFPR and issues are dealt with on a case-by-case basis, taking into account the degree of involvement of UTFPR-PG and EXA in the development or improvement of products, models or processes used. In addition to the above patent, a patent PIBR102017003311-2 has also been filed in the name of Atto Máquinas Ltda. for the MACHINE/PRODUCTION LINE FOR AUTOMATED HOSTAGE MANUFACTURING AND THE RESULTING PROCESS, which was the machine developed with funds from the Tecnova Project.

In 2015, the company built its own headquarters to house all the innovation projects and services (FIGURE 16). Following the Tecnova project in 2016, the need to better organise the company was noted, with a division of scopes and projects for better programming and execution of services. In this way, the company ATTO Máquinas was founded, focussing exclusively on the manufacture of wafer machines and the development of specific projects.

Figura 16   - Construction of own headquarters

Source: Images provided by the entrepreneur.

This has also enabled EXA to expand its market operations, developing electrical and automation projects; assembling electrical and pneumatic controls; developing, installing and maintaining industrial air conditioning, as well as designing and installing safety systems and complying with Regulatory Standard 12 (NR-12), which deals with safety when working with machinery and equipment (FIGURE 17).

automação elétrica

comércio e

manutenção

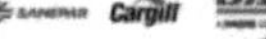

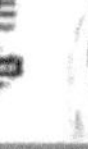

montagem de painéis elétricos
prestadora de serviços para SANEPAR

Figure 17 - Main services performed by EXA

Source: Images provided by the entrepreneur.

Providing automation services to other companies has also proved to be a promising business. It's about **"not putting all your eggs in one basket" (in the entrepreneur's view), providing services expands the possibilities of doing** business with other companies and makes it easier to pay the fixed costs of the business.In addition, EXA, through its entrepreneur, runs courses on the Regulatory Standards (NR10/NR33/NR35) issued by the Brazilian Ministry of Labour and Employment, which aim to guarantee the safety and health of workers who interact with installations and services in electricity, work at heights and confined spaces (FIGURE 18).

Figura 18 - Courses Taught

Source: Images provided by the entrepreneur.

EXA Automação's history of RD&I includes the development of specific machines according to customer needs, commercialisation and investment in innovation. Its main clients are Sanepar; Heineken; AP Winner; Brasswood; Arauco; LP Building; Continental; Águia Sistemas; DAF Caminhões; Bunge; Cargill, among others. These clients correspond to EXA's service market

In 2017, EXA had 30 (thirty) employees, including: industrial maintenance supervisors; designers; electricians; electromechanical technicians; administrative assistants; trainees in the areas of industrial automation technology and mechanics. Its physical facilities represent 80m^2 in the administrative area (administration, commercial, projects, warehouse, stock and finance), 70m2 in the production area (mechanical workshop and assembly of electrical panels) and it also has full *time* contract (third party companies) with 30m^2 in the workplace. In March 2017, EXA inaugurated its own headquarters with approximately 400m^2 . The company pays its employees fairly and also provides an additional bonus for specific tasks arising from projects involving the development of more complex technologies. Another aspect that stands out is its support for sports activities for employees and local institutions (FIGURE 19), including nature walks and football tournaments, among other activities.

Figura 19   - Sports Incentives

Source: Images provided by the entrepreneur.

In this respect, employees feel good about working for a company that cares about their health and well-being. In addition, the manager is always present at all activities, not only working together on operational routines but also supporting sports and leisure activities, which are organised by the employees themselves.

Exa received the award for best reference company (FIGURE 20) during **the "Entrepreneur's Fourth" cycle of business management consultancies, organised** by the Paraná Institute of Technology - Intec / Tecpar, the Paraná State Government and Finep, in November 2012.

Figura 20   - Best EXA Reference Company Award

Source: Images provided by the entrepreneur.

In addition, first EXA, now ATTO Máquinas is actively involved in the community, taking part in catechism classes where children are shown how the wafer is made and what it is made of (Figure 21).

Figura 21   - **Community involvement**
Source: Image provided by the entrepreneur.

CHAPTER 5

ECONOMIC, MARKET AND TECHNOLOGICAL CHALLENGES

The degree of innovation of the product developed can be considered a manufacturing process improvement, as its main characteristic is that it encompasses four different stages in one.

As a technological project, the new production line can be considered to be of medium technological complexity, namely: machine automation, programming
of the PLC (Programmable Logic Computer); study of different alloys of materials to develop the ideal temperature for the belt; control of the process, baking time, temperature and speed of the belt for greater productivity without losing quality; continuous belt system for baking the dough; process for automatic dosing of the dough (flour and water); humidification system in the continuous process and cutting of the particles (FIGURE 22 and FIGURE 23), in motion (continuous process).

MODELOS FABRICADOS ATUALMENTE
MÁQUINAS DE CORTE

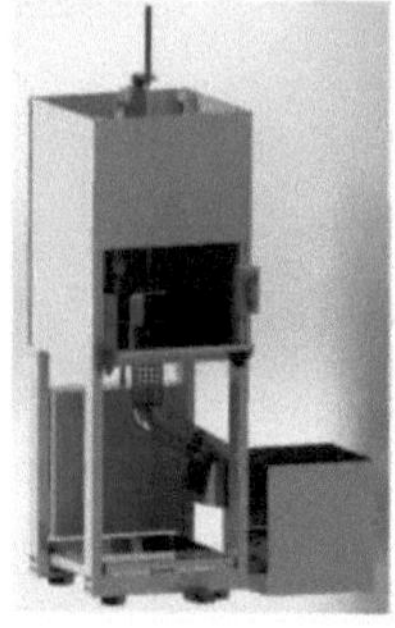

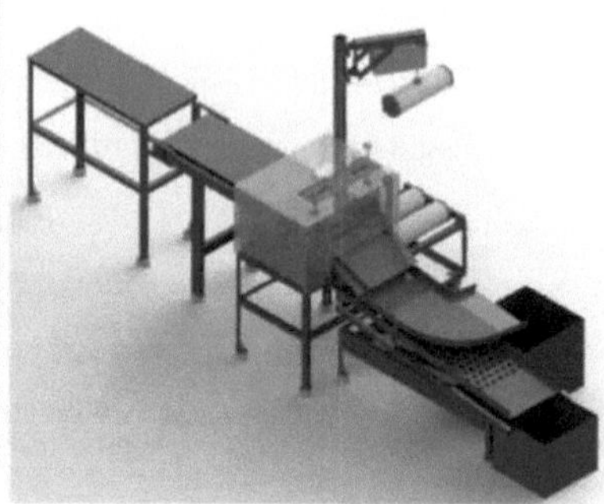

MODELOS FABRICADOS ATUALMENTE
UMIDIFICADORES

Figura 22 - **New models developed**

Source: Images provided by the entrepreneur.

Figura 23 **- New production line**
Source: Image provided by the entrepreneur.

The integration of all these stages, which require different time intervals for execution, establishes the need for fine tuning in their operation. The product's development stage is in the development of a 1:2 scale prototype, in which extremely satisfactory results have been obtained in all the stages described. In order to draw up the business plan, a study of competing companies was carried out (FIGURE 24) and it was noted that there are patents on the market for single-purpose machines and not for a wafer production line.

MAIORES CONCORRENTES MUNDIAIS

- Kissing-Menden – Alemanha – Fundada em 1850
- Formas Gimenez – Espanha – Fundada em 1902
- Officina Papini – Itália – Fundada em 1958

BRASIL

- Maq Company – Rio Claro - SP

COMPARATIVOS DE VALORES DAS MÁQUINAS

	MÁQUINA DE ASSAR MANUAL	MÁQUINA DE ASSAR SEMIAUTOMÁTICA
FABRICANTE	VALOR	VALOR
EXA AUTOMAÇÃO/ATTO MÁQUINAS	R$ 13.890,00	R$ 23.800,00
KISSING-MENDEN (Alemanha)	4.577,00 € - R$ 17.075,00	-
FORMAS GIMENEZ (Espanha)	12.600,00 € - R$ 46.998,00	19.300,00 € - R$ 71.989,00
OFFICINA PAPINI (Itália)	-	25.000,00 € - R$ 93.250,00

Utilizada cotação do dia 17/10/2017, na qual 1 € = R$ 3,73

Figura 24   - National and international competitors
Source: EXA (2018).

The manager says that technical and financial feasibility studies are constant in order to understand the market, competition, legislation and suppliers. Technological development, the provision of services to various medium and large companies, and EXA's own growth have required more and more people and an administrative structure compatible with the new **growth** prospects. **According to Theodoro: "It's getting difficult to** be responsible for everything, from buying to paying, from selling to receiving, from developing to manufacturing the product, from dream to reality, more people need to take part in this management dream." The machine developed is fully automatic, as shown in Figure 25.

Figura 25   - Automated wafer-making machine
Source: Image provided by the entrepreneur.

The competitive advantages of the product are that the machine developed is innovative, allowing for high productivity, minimising risks, low operating costs, quality of the end product, easy maintenance, and the company can offer a good system for technical assistance and customer service. With regard to the market, sales currently cover the local, regional and national markets, with a potential worldwide market. The entrepreneur says that potential customers are religious (convents, monasteries, dioceses, parishes, communities) who account for 40 per cent of production and lay people (companies that manufacture the particles for sale) who account for 60 per cent of production. There is only one competing company on the domestic market, but it has obsolete technology and low equipment productivity. On the international scene, there are factories in Mexico, Spain, Italy and Germany, but no manufacturer carries out all the production stages, as well as using obsolete and expensive technology.The expected results and benefits are considered in social terms through increased product quality, faster production, more satisfying work, reduced risks (accidents) and increased job creation; in economic terms through increased productivity, elimination of waste, cost reduction, increased business capacity, business growth and consolidation, improved company results; in environmental terms through optimised use of raw materials, lower energy and water consumption, reduced generation of industrial waste and in technical terms through more effective operational management and the use of reliable technology.Theodoro, in his entrepreneurial vision, believes in expanding the business to other activities in his area of expertise, betting on opening more companies (FIGURE 26).

Figura 26   - New companies

Source: Image provided by the entrepreneur.

Theodoro emphasises the company's growth:

> As the segment of wafer making machines is constantly growing, I thought it would be appropriate to open a new company, ATTO Máquinas Ltda. which is a specific company for the manufacture of wafer making machines. Recently, an opportunity arose in our city and I started a new branch of the electrical and pneumatic materials trade company called B2 Materiais elétricos e pneumáticos. As well as another company focused on developing electrical and automation projects, Dunamys Engenharia Elétrica, and most recently the acquisition of Zetta Climatização Industrial.

Figures 27 and 28 show the companies B2 Materiais Elétricos e Pneumáticos and Dunamys Automação Industrial, created in 2017.

Figura 27   - B2 Electrical and pneumatic materials

Source: Image provided by the entrepreneur.

Figura 28   - Dunamys Industrial Automation
Source: Image provided by the entrepreneur.

According to the manager, EXA Automação Industrial Ltda is aware of the challenges of positioning itself as a micro-enterprise and its need to innovate, given that its area of activity is technology-based and global market trends require pro-activity and continuous innovation.

With the creation of EXA Automação Industrial and successive acquisitions, the Dunexa group was formed (Figure 29), with significant results in the market.

Sonho

Hoje emprega mais de 70 colaboradores

Faturamento 2017 - 8 milhões de reais

Faturamento 2018 - previsto para 10 milhões

Figura 29   - DUNEXA Group companies

Source: Data provided by the entrepreneur.

Entrepreneur Theodoro is available to take part in events, talks, training sessions, courses, articles and more. Contacts can be made by email or telephone: + 55 42 9 9979-4644; theodoro@exa.ind.br.

Theodoro Bahniuk Neto
Diretor
Engenheiro Eletricista / Crea: PR - 99117/D

ANNEX 1 - TEACHING NOTES

CHAPTER 6

SUMMARY

This case study aims to analyse the development of the strategic management and innovation process at EXA. The sources of data collection are considered to be primary and secondary and a qualitative approach is adopted as the analysis procedure. The primary data collected was based on a semi-structured interview with the EXA manager. The secondary data was obtained from Exa Automação Industrial's website and is also based on documents and reports provided by the manager.

1 CASE APPLICATION

This teaching case can be applied to undergraduate subjects (entrepreneurship) and postgraduate *Lato Senso* subjects (Strategic Business Planning), applications that will be discussed below:

- Entrepreneurship - Undergraduate course

In undergraduate courses, this teaching case is used to discuss business opportunities for new entrepreneurs, differentiating between entrepreneurs who are looking for business opportunities and entrepreneurs who are looking for entrepreneurship out of necessity, i.e. people who have been made redundant, have taken part in voluntary redundancy processes, have received inheritances from parents and family members, among others. This case also points to the need to study the economic and financial viability of the business, analyse Michael Porter's competitive forces, the size of the market and the level of competition.

- Strategic Planning Course - Postgraduate Programme

In postgraduate studies, this teaching case is applied to discussions on the schools of strategic planning proposed by Mintzberg et al (2000), especially the school of organisational configuration and the adaptive model of Miles and Snow (1978), according to which organisations adapt their strategy and organisational structure to the environmental context in which they are inserted. From this perspective, the Miles and Snow (1978) model presents itself as a typology to be adopted in small and medium-sized companies, as a counterpoint to Michael Porter's strategies (Cost Strategy, Differentiation Strategy and Focus Strategy) traditionally applied in large organisations.

2 EDUCATIONAL OBJECTIVES

- Entrepreneurship - Undergraduate course

a)   Ability to analyse problem situations, checking, in the light of the theory studied, what type of problem has been presented and classifying it;

b)   Identify threats and opportunities for the market in which the entrepreneur intends to operate with their business idea.

- Strategic Planning Course - Postgraduate Programme

a)   Ability to analyse the case study in the light of the proposed theory, identifying characteristics in the teaching case that refute or confirm the theory under discussion;

b)   Ability to develop arguments and communicate ideas in group discussions;

c)   Ability to make connections between the theories analysed, indicating points of commonality and points of distance;

d) To develop the student's ability to analyse and synthesise the theories proposed.

3 ALTERNATIVES FOR ANALYSING THE CASE

In this case of teaching, it is recommended to plan the activity, taking into account the following aspects:

a)   Reading of the teaching case by the students, indicating central themes to be perceived by them and noted for future discussion;

b)   Formation of discussion groups, at the teacher's discretion, to analyse the perceptions shared by the group;

c)   Reading the indicated bibliography, where students must: (i) identify points of theory (typologies, taxonomies, classifications) that help them understand and solve the case study; (ii) summarise the main contributions of the text; (iii) compare the supporting texts, indicating their complementarity of elements or points of divergence;

d)   With these classifications and notes, the group can set about solving the questions posed by the activity, indicating: (i) the solution to the proposed problem; (ii) the theoretical justification; (iii) the factual justification based on the data in the text for the proposed problem; (iv) the inter-group discussion on the propositions made by each study group.

e)   The mediating teacher should: (i) read the case study; (ii) read the specified bibliography; (iii) draw up a summary of the case and the bibliography; (iv) check texts or videos that can complement the analysis, adding information, creating figures or diagrams that facilitate understanding of the problem, among others.

4 THE CONTRIBUTIONS OF MILES AND SNOW'S THEORY

The typology of strategic management styles formulated by Miles and Snow (1978) is based on three premises (FIGURE 1):

i)   companies develop a system for adapting and aligning with the external environment, also known as the adaptive cycle;

ii) four strategic styles emerge from analysing the environment: defenders, prospectors, analysts and reactors; and

iii) In this way, organisations have relative freedom to create their context, structure and strategy, which means that the level of organisational performance results from the consistency of these factors.

Figure 1 - Strategic positions in the competitive environment
Source: Adapted from Miles and Snow (1978).

For Arragón-Sanchez and Sánchez-Marín (2005), the typology of strategies formulated by Miles and Snow (1978) has important implications for business management, because depending on the management style (prospector, analyst, defender or reactive) adopted by the organisation, the company can emphasise management aspects involving technological positioning, the search for innovation, organisational design and human resource management.

Traditionally, studies on strategy have focussed on large companies, as Porter (1980), Ansoff (1979), Mintzberg et al (2006) and others have masterfully done. Miles and Snow's (1978) typology has been used to study small and medium-sized companies. According to the authors, the different strategic types vary depending on the innovations developed, as well as the technological position they occupy and/or develop in relation to their competitors. Another aspect highlighted involves the issue of flexibility and organisational design, which allow for greater speed of response, capacity for innovation and ability to adapt to change, not to mention aspects such as cooperation and human resource management.

Miles and Snow (1978) consider that managers make strategic choices based on their perceptions of the environment and the organisation's capabilities. Effective organisational adaptation depends on the ability of managers, not only to foresee and implement new forms of organisation, but also on the management of direct people and controls within organisations. The ability of managers to meet environmental conditions with future success revolves around their understanding of organisations as an integrated and dynamic whole. The authors emphasise that an analytical management style makes use of a traditional people management model, and this involves:

a) Assumptions: even if work is unpleasant for many people, what they do is less important than what they earn for doing it, few in the early stages of a business can manage and control themselves;

b) Policies: the manager's basic task is to control subordinates, determining their activities and obligations, establishing the organisation's work routines and procedures;

c) Expectations: people expect a decently paid job and a boss who is fair, work tends to be simple and controlled, where people have to produce what is expected of them.

This adaptation of strategy to the competitive environment was called **the "Adaptive Cycle" (FIGURE 2)** by the **authors Miles and Snow (1978, p. 24)** and its stages consist of the solutions given to the following problems:

a) *Entrepreneurial problem:* product-market mastery, success attitude, monitoring the environment and growth policy.

b) Technological or production *(engineering problem): technological* objectives, technological scope and technological orientation.

c) Administrative or structural *(administrative problem):* dominant administrative function, planning attitude, organisational structure and control.

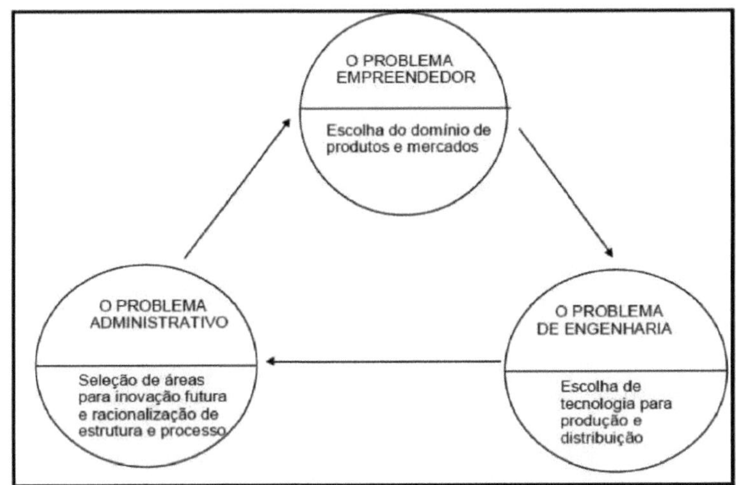

Figure 2 - The Adaptive Cycle

Source: Miles and Snow (1978, p. 24).

For Gurkov and Obel (2013), who carried out research into Miles and Snow's typology and its impact on the organisation's stakeholders, it is easy to see a change in management styles as the company grows and consolidates, the search for strategic stability, structural and product stability, stability in organisational design, makes organisations become reactive and/or analytical, but this does not mean that they are giving up innovation, in fact the cost of change becomes higher, the stakeholders in the strategy have more power and influence over the organisation's decisions. In this way, much more effort is put into processes of anticipating change, planning change, creating projects and teams responsible for change. When the organisation is in its initial stages, change can be more instinctive, rapid, effective and constant.

Soares et al (2011) related Miles and Snow's typology to organisational behaviour in companies in the hotel sector in Florianópolis - SC, where they identified factors such as: the existence of a dominant coalition in the organisation, the existence of a perception of this coalition in relation to change, the segmentation of opinions, ways of monitoring the external and internal environment, as well as dynamic restrictions that change systematically, making organisational change difficult.

For Gimenez et al (1999) the four types of strategy identified by Miles and Snow (1978) differ in the way some of the dimensions of entrepreneurial, engineering and administrative problems are solved (TABLE 1), as well as the potential problems that impact on strategy and this involves:

a)   the failure of management to articulate a viable organisational strategy;

b)   the strategy is articulated, but technology, structure and processes are not adequately

41

linked to it; or

c)   management adheres to a particular association between strategy and structure, despite the fact that the latter is no longer relevant in environmental conditions (GIMENEZ et al, 1999, p. 60).

Table 1: Dimensions of the adaptive cycle, characteristics and strategic types

Components of Adaptive Cycle	Dimensions	STRATEGIC TYPES			
		Defensive	Prospector	**_Analítira_**	Reactive
Problem Contractor and Solutions	Dnmmin of products and markets	Narrow and carefully focused	Large and expanding	Segmented and carefully adjusted	Irregular and transitory
	Posture of success	Prominent in its market	Active initiation of change	Careful followers of change	Opportunistic investments and adaptation posture
	Environmental monitoring	Domain-based and careful/strong organisational monitoring	Market and environment orientated - aggressive search	Competition-orientated and complete	Sporadic and dominated by specific topics
	Growth	Careful penetration and productivity advances	Product and market development and diversification	Assertive penetration and careful product and market development	Hasty changes
Problem of **Engineering** Solutions	Technological objective	Cost efficiency	Flexibility and innovation	Synergy Secnoiógira	Project development and awareness
	Technological breadth	Single, focal technology;' basic _expertise_	Multiple technologies advancing in the future	Interrelating technologies on the border	Changeable technological applications/ Fluidity
	Technological bulkheads	Maintenance and standardisation programmes	Technical staff skills." diversity	Increnaenialism and synergy	Ability to experiment and improvise solutions
Administrative Problems and Solutions	Dominant coalition	Finance and Promotion	Marketing r R&D	Staff Planning	Solutions problems
	Planning	From the inside out' dominated by control	Search for problems and opportunities -' perspective of programmes or campaigns	Comprehensive with incremental changes	Crisis-orientated and disjointed
	Structure	Functional/ Line authority	By products and'or markets	Advisor-dominated / matrix-orientated	Rigid formal authority / loose operational frown
	Control	Centralised, formal and anchored in financial aspects	Performance in the market-' sales volume	Multiple methods" careful risk calculations" sales contribution	Avoid problems.' solve remaining problems

Source: Gimenez et al (1999, p. 61).

Gimenez et al (1999) state, according to the organisational strategy analysis model proposed by Miles and Snow (1978), that the company that adopts this strategy falls between the defensive and prospecting strategies by maintaining a limited line of relatively stable products/services, while at the same time trying to add one or more new products/services that have been successful in other companies in the sector.

According to Vasconcelos et al (2007), the strategy adopted by small and medium-sized companies is strongly influenced, if not totally defined, by their owner-managers, i.e. business behaviour derives from the behaviour of their managers. For a better understanding of strategies, the authors have drawn up a summary table, see table 2, with some characteristics of each strategic type.

In their studies, the authors state that more important than strategically framing a particular style, there is a pressing need for managers/leaders to prepare the organisation for change. An organisation's business becomes more efficient and effective as a result of its ability to perceive the need for change, reading and monitoring the external environment, adapting and flexibilising products, technology, services, structure and organisational behaviour to the new environmental reality, and this can be considered the best way for a company to survive and develop.

Table 2: Strategic typologies and characterisation

Strategic typology	Characterisation
Detensive Strategy	Companies that adopt this type of strategy: - Maintain a relatively stable product/service line - They have a close command of the product and the market - They don't tend to look for new opportunities outside their domain - Managers are highly specialised in their field - 0 control and decision-making are centralised - Strategic actions are aimed at securing a share of the market by offering better quality products, superior services and/or lower prices.
Prospect strategy	A company that adopts this strategy: - Looking for new business opportunities, continually seeking to expand its range of products/services - Their managers are highly flexible when it comes to change and innovation - Business activities are decentralised.
Analytical Strategy	A company that follows this strategy: - It endeavours to maintain a limited line of relatively stable products/services and at the same time tries to add one or more new products/services that have been successful in other companies in the sector; - They protect the stable potion of their market - 0 control and decision-making is centralised; however, it is possible to identify flexibility in actions.
Reactive Strategy	The company that adopts a reactive strategy - They lack the ability to respond effectively to the implications of changes in their environment; - Does not take risks on new products/services unless threatened by competitors; - 0 control and decision-making are highly centralised; - The organisational structure is rigid.

Source: Vasconcelos et al (2007, p. 126).

Another aspect to be analysed involves analysing Miles and Snow's typology from the point of view of the schools of strategic planning proposed by Mintzberg et al (2000), where the typology fits into the Configuration School. In this school, according to Fernandes (2007), organisations are analysed as clusters of characteristics and behaviours, whose members each develop their own strategy, integrating and taking advantage of the contributions of the other schools.

Miles and Snow (1978) helped not only to launch the configurational view of strategy, but also to crystallise the concept of strategic equifinality. According to Doty et al. (1993) and Hambrick (2003), the idea of strategic equifinality considers that, in a given industry or environment, there is more than one way to prosper, although there are not an infinite number of possibilities. In other words, this model of analysis seeks to assess organisational adaptation to changes in the environment by studying the relationship between strategy, structure and processes.

5 QUESTIONS TO DISCUSS THE CASE IN CLASS

- Entrepreneurship - Undergraduate course

a) Does Theodoro work from a perspective of entrepreneurship by necessity or opportunity? Indicate aspects of the text that demonstrate your answer.

To resolve this question, we recommend reading the text by SCHNEIDER, E.I.; CASTELO BRANCO, H.J. A Caminhada Empreendedora: a jornada de transformação dos sonhos em realidade. Curitiba: Editora Intersaberes, 2011, chapter 01, p. 17-36.

From the authors' perspective, an entrepreneur is someone who does something, mobilising resources and taking risks to start businesses and/or organisations. Therefore, when an individual or group of individuals undertakes entrepreneurship, they do so from two perspectives: Opportunity or Necessity.

Entrepreneurs by necessity, as the name suggests, are driven by necessity, the entrepreneurial journey is often driven by the lack of satisfactory alternatives for occupation and income. Another possibility comes from family ties: fathers, uncles and relatives may have been entrepreneurs, even if they didn't have the vocation or desire to become one, when they receive an inheritance they may find themselves in the role of entrepreneur and/or business manager.

Business opportunity entrepreneurs, on the other hand, are those who do so in a planned, thought-out way, based on reason and economic/financial studies that determine the potential of a given entrepreneurial opportunity.

In this teaching case, Theodoro represents an entrepreneur by opportunity, who pursues entrepreneurship out of a desire to be a business owner, who studies, researches, looks for niches and opportunities that can be utilised with his technical management skills acquired in higher education.

- Strategic Planning Course - Postgraduate Programme

b) Theodoro's persistence in pursuing the technical and economic viability of the company indicates what management style? Reactive, Defensive, Analytical or Prospective?

To resolve this question, we recommend reading the text by: GIMENEZ, F.A.P.; PELISSON, C.; KRUGER, E. G.S. HAYASHI JR, P.; Estratégia em Pequenas Empresas: uma Aplicação do Modelo de Miles e Snow. RAC, v. 3, n. 2, May/Aug. 1999: 53-74

For Gimenez et al (1999), the organisational strategy analysis model proposed by Miles and Snow (1978) has been well accepted in small business studies, where the entrepreneur who creates the business is primarily responsible for strategy. From this perspective, Theodoro's management style at EXA can be considered Analytical, where:

A company that follows this strategy tries to maintain a limited line of relatively stable products/services and at the same time tries to add one or more new products/services that have been successful in other companies in the sector. In many ways it is an intermediate position between the defensive and prospecting strategies (GIMENEZ et al, 2008, p.30).

These characteristics can be found in the following aspects of this case study:

I - The search for business opportunities, duly studied and analysed, with a view to making the best possible decision. Take the first discarded product idea, for example;

II-   The search for partnerships with other companies to provide services and develop technical solutions for these organisations, seeking new sources of revenue and stability for the business;

III-   Investment in the development of the wafer production line on the basis of an investment project carried out with the funding bodies;

IV-   Search for incentive programmes for starting a business, the incubator, industrial development areas proposed by the municipality, among others.

c) Can EXA's strategic decisions, and Theodoro's as a result, be explained in the light of Miles and Snow's adaptive cycle theory?

To resolve this question, we recommend reading MILES, R. E.; SNOW, C. C. Organisational strategy, structure and process. New York: McGraw-Hill, 1978.

Miles and Snow (1978) consider that managers make strategic choices based on their perceptions of the environment and the organisation's capabilities. Effective organisational adaptation depends on the ability of managers, not only to foresee and implement new forms of organisation, but also on the management of direct people and controls within organisations. We believe that managers' ability to successfully meet tomorrow's environmental conditions revolves around their understanding of organisations as an integrated and dynamic whole.

In this proposal, for the authors, an analytical management style, as set out in the first question, makes use of a traditional people management model, and this involves:

I - Assumptions: even if work is unpleasant for many people, what they do is less important than what they earn for doing it, few in the early stages of a business can manage and control themselves;

II - Policies: the manager's basic task is to control subordinates, determining their activities and obligations, establishing the organisation's work routines and procedures;

III - Expectations: people expect a decently paid job and a boss who is fair, work tends to be simple and controlled, where people have to produce what is expected of them.

Analysing the case of EXA, people must feel good about working for the company, because the presence of the manager collaborating in operational activities, directing tasks, given the small number of employees, contributes with his expertise as a technologist and engineer in operations that require high technology above all, and employees are supported in their activities by being paid a fair wage and receiving an additional fee when carrying out projects that involve this cutting-edge technology. Another aspect is the company's concern for employee health and well-being, providing leisure and relaxation activities that certainly contribute to increased productivity and quality of service.

d) When analysing the decisions from the point of view of the adaptive cycle (Entrepreneur, Engineering and Structure (administrative)) compared to the management style (Reactive, Defender, Analytical, Prospector) can we say that a single style was adopted? Has the management style changed in the different stages of the cycle?

To resolve this question, we recommend reading MILES, R. E.; SNOW, C. C. Organisational strategy, structure and process. New York: McGraw-Hill, 1978.

Although the entrepreneur showed innovative characteristics in the search for new business opportunities, his main style involves a more analytical stance, one of planned change, with careful risk calculations from an administrative point of view.

In this sense, EXA is the creator of the wafer making machine and seeks to serve its customers by diversifying its operations with other services and products similar to the fully automatic wafer making machine, at a lower cost, such as the manual wafer making machine and the simple pneumatic wafer making machine. In addition to diversifying its manufacturing operations, it also sells and maintains electrical, hydraulic and pneumatic machines for industrial use and provides services in the preparation of industrial automation projects. It also sells electrical and pneumatic products, provides industrial maintenance services and adapts machines to NR-12 standards, among other services.

From the point of view of the entrepreneur, who is looking for products for segmented markets, orientated towards competition, assertive penetration and the careful development of products and markets. From an engineering point of view, his style can be considered prospector, as he seeks flexibility and innovation, technologies that can be combined, taking advantage of his technical knowledge.

In this way, it can be inferred that the management style of the small company is more flexible, adapting to the characteristics and reality of the market encountered. It is therefore necessary to analyse the whole and check which of these characteristics are most marked, in Theodoro's case the analyst style, because EXA operates in the market with caution, calculating and minimising the risks of the business without failing to invest in new technology in the development of new products and also offering services in its area of activity, in order to serve its customers.

e) Is there alignment between the chosen strategy and the organisational processes and structures?

To resolve this question, we recommend reading the text by MINZBERG, Henry; AHLSTRAND, Bruce; LAMPEL, Joseph. Strategy Safari: a roadmap through the jungle of strategic planning. Porto Alegre: Bookman, 2000 and the text by MILES, R. E.; SNOW, C. C. Organisational strategy, structure and process. New York: McGraw-Hill, 1978.

Miles and Snow observed the interrelationships of the various attributes: product/market behaviour with entry, technology, structure and management processes. Organisations that follow these strategies develop certain consistency mechanisms and tend to perpetuate that strategy. The positive side of this conclusion is that organisations cope well and respond positively to the external environment; the negative side is that organisations find it difficult to accept that they need to change, or to implement organisational change.

Analysing the EXA case, as the company has sought to develop its physical structure and people, it is also growing. It should be noted that the product and service line is also beginning to be designed, with innovation on the one hand and standardised services on the other, combining stability and novelty in the business context. In this sense, EXA's organisational strategy, in its complexity, prepares the organisation for a systemic reaction, reconfiguring the organisation

whenever necessary, as advocated by Miles and Snow's adaptive model.

By adopting the strategy of trying to reach international markets by devising and developing a state-of-the-art machine, it seeks to combine the strengths and opportunities of the external environment in terms of investments and resources from calls for proposals, thereby boosting its innovation process. Another aspect is the strategy aimed at protecting knowledge by granting patents, guaranteeing its know-how in the manufacture of a fully automated machine. Therefore, it endeavours to focus on the internal environment, processes and people, as well as the external environment, the international market and financing policies, in order to guarantee the perpetuation of its business.

The main results identify the entrepreneur's management traits in the face of business opportunities. The manager has the capacity for effective organisational adaptation, not only to predict and implement new forms of management processes, but also to manage people and the company's internal controls. The adaptive model studied offers a theory that allowed the company to be understood and analysed. It can be concluded that the management style of a small company is more flexible, adapting to the characteristics and reality of the market encountered, and the whole must be analysed to identify the most striking characteristics.

REFERENCES

ANSOFF, H.I. **Strategic management**. London: Macmillan, 1979.

ARRAGÓN-SANCHEZ, A.; SÁNCHEZ-MARÍN, G. Strategic orientation, management characteristics and performance: a study of Spanish SMEs. **Journal of Small Business Management**, v. 43, n. 3, p. 287-308, Jul. 2005.

DORNELAS, J. C. A. **Empreendedorismo:** transformando ideias em negócios. Rio de Janeiro: Elsevier, 2001.

DOTY, D. H., GLICK, W. H., HUBER, G. P. Fit, equifinality, and organisational effectiveness: A test of two configurational theories. **Academy of Management Journal**, 36(6), 1993: 1196-1250.

DRUCKER, P. F. **Innovation and entrepreneurship**: practice and principles. Cengage Learning Editores, 2014.

EXA. Exa Industrial Automation. Available at: http://www.exa.ind.com.

FERNANDES, A. Dimensão integrativa do planeamento estratégico. **Brazilian and Portuguese Journal of Management**, March 2007.

FIZZ, P. C. Building better causal theories: a Fuzzy set approach to typologies in organisation research. **Academy of Management Journal**, April 2011.

GIMENEZ, F. A., PELISSON, C., KRUGER, E. G., HAYASHI Jr, P. Estratégia em pequenas empresas: uma aplicação do modelo de Miles e Snow. **Revista de Administração Contemporânea**, RAC, v. 3, n. 2, May/Aug. 1999: 53-74.

GURKOV, I., OBEL, B. Revisiting Miles-Snow typology of strategic orientation using stakeholder theory. ICOA Working Papers Series, **AARHUSS University Business and Social Sciences**, 2013.

HAMBRICK, D. On the staying power of defenders, analysers, and prospectors. **Academy of Management Executive**, vol. 17, n. 4, 2003: 115-118.

HAROLD, D.; GLICK, W.; HUBER, G.; Fit, equifinality, and organisational effectiveness: A test. **Academy of Management Journal**, vol. 36, n. 6, 1993.

MCCLELLAND, D. C. Toward a theory of motivational acquisition. **American Psychologist**, 20(5), 321, 1965.

MILES, R. E.; SNOW, C. C. **Organisational strategy, structure and process**. New York: McGraw-Hill, 1978.

MINTZBERG, H. L., AHLSTRAND, B., LAMPEL, J. **Strategy Safari**. Porto Alegre: Bookman Editora, 2009.

MINTZBERG, H. L.; LAMPEL, J.; QUINN, J.B.; GHOSHAL, S. **The strategy process:** concepts, contexts and selected cases. Porto Alegre: Bookman, 2006.

PORTER, M. E. **Competitive strategy:** techniques for analysing industries and competitors. New York: Free Press, 1980.

SCHNEIDER, E.I.; CASTELO BRANCO, H.J. **A caminhada empreendedora:** a jornada de transformação dos sonhos em realidade. Curitiba: Editora Intersaberes, 2011: 17-36.

SCHUMPETER, J. A. **The theory of economic development**: An enquiry into profits, capital, credit, interest, and the business cycle;[Transl. of the 2. German ed.]. Oxford University Press, 1961.

SOARES, M. L.; TEIXEIRA, O. R. P.; PELISSARI, A. S. Organisational behaviour: an application of Miles and Snow's typology in the hotel sector of Florianópolis - SC. **Revista de Administração da Universidade Federal de Santa Maria,** vol. 4, núm. 2, May-August, 2011, pp. 251-267.

VASCONCELOS, A.C.F.;GUEDES, I.A.; CÂNDIDO, G.A. Application of the Miles and Snow and Kirton model in small and medium-sized enterprises: an exploratory study. GERPROS. **Production, Operations and Systems Management.** Year 2, vol. 3, May-June 2007, p. 123-132.

WILDAUER, E.W. **Business plan:** constituent elements and preparation process. Curitiba: Intersaberes, 2012.

I want morebooks!

Buy your books fast and straightforward online - at one of world's fastest growing online book stores! Environmentally sound due to Print-on-Demand technologies.

Buy your books online at
www.morebooks.shop

Kaufen Sie Ihre Bücher schnell und unkompliziert online – auf einer der am schnellsten wachsenden Buchhandelsplattformen weltweit! Dank Print-On-Demand umwelt- und ressourcenschonend produziert.

Bücher schneller online kaufen
www.morebooks.shop